Independent Filmmaking: The Ultimate Guide

Written by Ricky Burchell

Contents

Introduction

The term 'independent filmmaking' applies to any film that is made outside of a major studio system. You wouldn't look at a Disney film and consider it to be an 'indie' film, as it has a massive name behind it and has been produced by a conglomerate organization that owns many other franchises, estates and much more. Independent filmmaking is all about creating something outside of the mainstream blockbuster channels - and with that, often means having a much smaller budget and a lot more to lose if it goes wrong (in terms of your time and resources - financially your losses would be smaller than that of a Disney failure, but the personal loss is greater).

'Indie' itself is a term that has been coined by filmmakers, film critics and audience members alike to describe this, but there's much more to the label than simply that. Indie films themselves can even be, and have been, considered a genre in themselves [1] - often working to similar size budgets, using similar locations as costs need to be kept to a minimum and often being story-centric, homing in on character and plot development over costly CGI and impressive set pieces.

In *Independent, Mainstream and In Between: How and Why Indie Films Have Become Their Own Genre*, Carrie Szabo describes the rise of independence in the film industry, highlighting the anti-Hollywood approach to filmmaking that emerged and how the definition of the term 'independent' really wasn't as clear cut as it is today.

"By the late-1950s "independent" shifted to mean something else than what it

meant thirty years prior. In 1956, 53 percent of films distributed by ex-studios, 'were deemed 'independent', since those major companies had not actually made the films, they only distributed them" [1].

Filmmakers with financial help from studios, who were directing and producing their own work, were still being considered independent. But really, just how independent was the production of those films, when you're relying on somebody else for the cash? Most people today would argue this point.

Janet Wasko provides an insightful definition of independent filmmaking. Still, a very different approach to the topic today. It was obvious that by the mid-to-late 50s, the term seemed to be open to interpretation, rather than having a fixed definition of what exactly independent really meant for the film industry.

"The independent producer included the single picture company, the 'small

operator' who made cheap quickies, and the established producer who continuously produced 'quality' films at the major studios, or at their own studios" [1].

It was only by the early 1960s that the anti-Hollywood movement gained any traction. Szabo describes the emerging movement as something greater than the non-mainstream approaches that had previously been taken. Calling it 'New American Cinema'.

All of a sudden, filmmakers were able to free themselves from the over-professionalism, the over-technicality and the sometimes-unjustifiable limitations set by big business in Hollywood. Creativity and freedom could finally be achieved in perfect harmony - they could now guide themselves using their experience and knowledge of the industry, rather than going 'exactly by the book', following exactly what an executive at a studio wanted the film to be. The filmmaker could throw those limitations out the window.

Aspects such as improvised dialogue were more commonly used, with Americans adapting what they were seeing from French New Wave cinema [1]. Handheld cameras were another aspect that the Americans were drawing inspiration from, utilizing it if it was to work effectively for their creative piece - contemporary editing techniques from French New Wave were also implemented. Without the limitations that big business Hollywood had, independent filmmakers were able to try new things.

An un-Hollywood aesthetic is what these filmmakers were striving to achieve, whether they achieved it by using purposely rough editing techniques, off-kilter characterization, quirky soundtrack choices or even something else. American filmmakers of the time (the ones striving to achieve uniqueness) were living by the philosophy "Do your own thing!".

And this point still stands today. Independent filmmaking has strived to achieve that vision ever since. Independent filmmakers dare to be different, opting to take an alternative approach, tackle subjects others may view as taboo - and make those surprising creative choices you're likely to never see from companies like Disney or Sony.

Independent filmmakers should be visionaries if they are to succeed, as you won't get far trying to do a low-budget version of Spider-Man. Be bold, stand out, dare to be different and reach for the stars - but before you do, make sure you read this guide, as we hope it will be of great use to you as you begin your journey in the independent filmmaking business.

Throughout this book, we'll cover all aspects of the independent filmmaking process - including what to expect afterwards and what you probably should consider when your film is done and distributed.

We'll be taking an in-depth look at the following steps in the independent filmmaking process;

The Script

Without a good script, you're not going to find much success. Before you ever put a script into production, always make sure it's the best it can possibly be - and yes, that probably means sharing the script with more than just your friends and your parents. As harsh as it may sound, they are likely to lie to you even if they think it's the worst thing they've ever read. We'll be taking a closer look at this in the upcoming chapter 'The Script' - so if you have areas of concern surrounding only the script, or you'd just like to find out more, skip ahead.

Pre-Production

Covering various aspects before you hit the record button. This can be a daunting phase of the independent filmmaking process, as it all starts to feel real (that's because it is, you're going to be making a movie soon).

Production

You've hit the record button and you're well on your way to creating something fantastic (or at least you hope you are). In this section of the book, we'll take a look at the various aspects of the production phase that you need to get spot on, including what to expect and the potential problems that may arise.

Post Production

Everything from editing to the final cut, the hard part is done by this point, right? Wrong. Every step of the process is important, read more to find out why.

What Comes Next?

Not only are we covering what exactly you should expect from the independent filmmaking process, but we'll be taking a look at what to do after you've finished and distributed your first indie film.

If that all sounds like your cup of tea (or coffee, if that's what you're into), enjoy the book and make the most of the information. Oh, and if you happen to make a very successful film that wins awards, we'd like a mention or two in your acceptance speech. Just kidding, maybe?

Your Career

Independent filmmaking isn't exactly something you're pushed towards at school. When you talk about careers, particularly when you reach your teens, you'll often hear teachers pushing more secure career paths. It's not that they don't believe that being an independent filmmaker isn't a career, it's simply because it can be a risky path to take.

In Terry Green's article for Filmmaker, titled *Independent Filmmaking: Passion Or Profession?* he talks about the various aspects of a filmmakers career, exploring how exactly we should look at it - and whether or not we can actually make enough money from it to warrant calling it a profession [2].

"Independent filmmaking as we know it isn't what it once was, when stepping behind the camera meant you had arrived at a certain level and achieved a certain distinction in your career. Directing movies was once reserved for those who had made previous achievements in the industry and earned their way into the director's chair" [2].

In his quote, Terry Green makes a valid point, highlighting (as we did in our Introduction) that the definition of the role has changed. Even in the anti-Hollywood age, the right of an independent filmmaker came from experience, and expertise - you had to have achievements behind you in order to stand a chance.

With the wider availability of film equipment, the dirt cheap to the most expensive equipment (ranging from low budget to Hollywood standard), it's easy to put yourself in the filmmakers position - even if you have no experience whatsoever. We're not here to say you're any less of a filmmaker because you don't have the same experience as a small-time director working with a small studio, or even a top Hollywood director like Christopher

Nolan. We're just pointing out that the goalposts have moved in the film industry - giving just about anybody with a willingness to learn, the opportunity to become a filmmaker.

Now, it's important to note this isn't an easy job - regardless of what equipment you have and the script you have behind you, there's nothing to suggest you're definitely going to succeed. You can have all the tools, but if you don't have the appropriate skills to use them effectively, you unfortunately won't get far.

"Today, a hand-held digital camera and home editing system is all you need to make a film and to call yourself a director — a few thousand dollars out of pocket and you're on your way" [2].

'So, what does this actually mean for independent filmmakers?' you might be asking. Well, as we've discussed above, it's a lot easier for people to go out and try their hand at filmmaking. It's worth noting too, that these may be people who decades ago would have never had the opportunity to. Due to the technology and smaller costs involved with production today, they are now able to give it a go.

Terry Green makes an interesting counter argument, stating that now there is so much out there in terms of volume, it has watered down the landscape - making it much harder to recognize actual talent. The current landscape of independent filmmaking, due to the sheer volume being pumped out on a daily basis (largely due to the world's huge population with access to film equipment), is allowing actual talent to go unrecognized as film after film get released too little to no recognition.

Later, Terry Green goes on to explain how he's certain of one thing - the above has made it very difficult for people to define independent filmmaking as a genuine, viable occupation. It's easy to see his point, with so much competition out there - and knowing just how much work goes into a typical independent film, is there really any money to be made in the business?

It appears unlikely, but that goes for the film industry in general, until you find a way in, you're stuck just looking for a means of paying the bills. In the world of film, you have to persevere - and giving it time does not suggest it's never going to happen. Sometimes having patience is key, providing there's enough fire in your belly to keep you motivated.

But, we know it's hard to stay motivated when the money dries up and you're actively pursuing a career as an independent filmmaker. We have included the following quote from Terry Green, not to discourage you from entering the world of independent filmmaking - but as a means of motivating you to prove him wrong.

"In this film economy. The best they [independent filmmakers] could hope for was admission into one of the hundreds of film festivals that have cropped up in recent years — where their visions might gain ground and their film careers might get launched" [2].

So, don't just reach for admission into one of those talked about film festivals, strive for admission in many, strive to get your work noticed - strive to make every decision you've made in your independent filmmaking career really worth it.

Like we mentioned, the world of independent. filmmaking is not an easy one - but providing you've got the stomach for it and you're willing to fight to express yourself creatively, project your vision and inspire others - you'll already be well on your way to success.

The Industry

When you tell people you're entering the film industry (in whatever form it may be, whether it's as a researcher on a daytime TV series or a scriptwriter for a popular TV series), you'll often hear the same thing.

'The film industry is a fickle one' - or something like that. To give them credit, they're certainly right, there's no arguing that. But, does it mean you shouldn't push for a career in the industry? Definitely not. Go out and achieve your dreams, no matter what they are.

So, what exactly is this fickle industry all about? Let's take a look;

The first, and obvious answer that most people with good, honest souls will think of is 'the vision'. The film industry is all about getting your message out there in a creative way that is well received, or at least it should be.

In theory, it's all about the idea, it's all about the good reviews and making sure the audience you were trying to appeal to get the point of your film and enjoy it, but there's so much more to it than that. Unfortunately, it all boils down to, you guessed it, money.

Budget and projected box office earnings are everything in mainstream cinema, reviews and general audience reception not so much. When it comes to larger productions, where hundreds of people can be involved in the production of a film at any given time, it's easy to see why projected box office figures mean everything to big studios - they need to be making profitable films in order to flourish. Too many box office flops can cripple any film studio.

So, with the industry as it is, it's more important than ever to not only consider your idea but think of it as somebody in business. Is your idea profitable? Does it have franchise potential? Who are the target audience? Why would your target audience want to watch this film? Why would anybody want to watch this film? What do you do with your film that hasn't been done in previous works within the same genre? What inspired your film? Is it too close to the story that inspired it?

Too many questions for you? That's only the start!

Unfortunately, though it's so easy to simply think of the film industry from a creative standpoint, you need to put on your business hat throughout the entire creative process - thinking about how and why your film could fly. Why people would bother to go and see it, for instance. Business and creativity go hand in hand in the film industry, it's important to understand that before you even begin to think about the script.

And when money is so important in the film industry, you've got to consider those people higher up (particularly in Hollywood) are willing to make drastic decisions in order to get the job done for the price they want to pay - ensuring they have the best chance of hitting those high box office numbers. Hence why people say the film industry is a fickle one. The ever-changing nature of the industry, including the ever-shifting job roles (directors given the boot from certain projects) and the frequent feelings of betrayal, all validate the 'fickle' arguments.

But, this is bound to happen when money is the main concern. Money makes the world go 'round - and it certainly keeps the film industry afloat. See, it would be rare to find someone in any position of power in the film industry that's agenda wasn't to make money.

But what about the film industry in relation to independent filmmaking?

Firstly, be prepared for stiff competition. Mainstream culture and viewing habits are hard to change, so don't go into the independent filmmaking business expecting to be recognized immediately for your talent. Certainly, don't expect audiences to flock to your film over Fast and Furious 9 either, as it just won't happen. Indie films are a whole other beast, it's unlikely you'll ever have the budget to tackle a mainstream blockbuster during your independent filmmaking career - but this is your opportunity to stand out, showing why you're better than those corny action flicks.

The industry is ever changing - we can almost guarantee that if you were to read this book ten years after its publication date that something will have changed. But ride the beast we call the film industry for as long as you can and

make your message as strong as you can.
That's how to handle the film industry.

Inspiration

As a filmmaker, you'll likely draw inspiration from many other filmmakers, writers, speakers, music and life itself. Inspiration can be found in so many ways and you'll probably notice that there are things that you are inspired by that didn't even make it into our very condensed list.

Whether you're inspired by your favorite director's first feature film, or you're inspired by your writer's first big break on television, we all have something we can turn to that motivates us - usually because someone or a group of people have shown determination in the face of adversity.

Many find it useful to draw inspiration from several artists within the genres they're most interested in. For instance; let's say you like science fiction, you may draw inspiration from Steven Spielberg (for his work on many projects, from E.T. to Ready Player One), Joss Whedon (for his work on Firefly) and Ridley Scott (for Alien and Blade Runner).

Broadening your horizons and opening yourself up too many interpretations within the genres you're looking to work in is useful. It allows you to think more creatively and see exactly what other people have already done - so you can approach ways of doing it better.

In this chapter, we want to give you some words of wisdom from some of the great creative minds throughout history - hoping to further inspire you as you make your journey in the world of independent filmmaking.

"Pick up a camera. Shoot something. No matter how small, no matter how cheesy, no matter whether your friends and your sister star in it. Put your name on it as director. Now you're a director. Everything after that you're just negotiating your budget and your fee" [3].

– James Cameron

"When given an opportunity, deliver excellence and never quit".

— Robert Rodriguez

"The saddest journey in the world is the one that follows a precise itinerary. Then you're not a traveller. You're a f@@king tourist".

— Guillermo del Toro

"We don't make movies to make money, we make money to make more movies".

– Walt Disney

"Film is, to me, just unimportant. But people are very important".

— John Cassavetes

"Let me just pause a minute and drink in this moment. And if you film it, I'll be able to get free refills for life".

— Jarod Kintz

"Cinema is a matter of what's in the frame and what's out".

— Martin Scorsese

"There are no rules in filmmaking. Only sins. And the cardinal sin is dullness".

– Frank Capra

"The characters in my films try to live honestly and make the most of the lives they've been given. I believe you must live honestly and develop your abilities to the full. People who do this are the real heroes".

– Akira Kurosawa

"If there's specific resistance to women making movies, I just choose to ignore that as an obstacle for two reasons: I can't change my gender, and I refuse to stop making movies".

– Kathryn Bigelow

"A story should have a beginning, a middle, and an end… but not necessarily in that order".

– Jean-Luc Godard

"A film is – or should be – more like music than like fiction. It should be a progression of moods and feelings. The theme, what's behind the emotion, the meaning, all that comes later".

– Stanley Kubrick

"The Biggest Mistake in Student Films is That They Are Usually Cast So Badly, With Friends and People the Directors Know".

– **Brian De Palma**

"Although I Write Screenplays, I Don't Think I'm a Good Writer".

– **George Lucas**

"A lot of times you get credit for stuff in your movie that you didn't intend to be there".

– **Spike Lee**

"People say I pay too much attention to the look of a movie but for God's sake, I'm not producing a Radio 4 Play for Today, I'm making a movie that people are going to look at".

– **Ridley Scott**

"I think audiences get too comfortable and familiar in today's movies. They believe everything they're hearing and seeing. I like to shake that up"

– Christopher Nolan

"My idea of professionalism is probably a lot of people's idea of obsessive".

– David Fincher

The Idea

It probably goes without saying that the idea is one of the most important, if not the most important aspect of the filmmaking process. There's understandably a lot of pressure when it comes to your vision for what the idea should be.

These questions should be running through your mind.

- Will the audience like the idea?
- Will the audience get the idea?
- Is the idea different enough?
- Is this definitely going to stand out for the right reasons?

- Has the idea been created for me, or am I creating this for other people?

There are way more questions you should be asking yourself when it comes to the idea, but these are just a few in order to get the wheels in your head turning. As mentioned earlier in this guide, it's important to consider budget and how much money you expect to earn from this film when creating the idea. It needs to be targeted enough to get people interested but without compromising on the integrity of the story.

It's a difficult balance, but that's what makes the idea process so fun. You can write something, analyse it, see if it works, then go back regardless and make it stronger. You'll probably notice that in the idea development process, second, third, fourth and maybe even fifth drafts of your idea will lead to further idea generation, where you build on what you've already got.

This way, you can make the idea as strong as you can to the best of your abilities. It's probably important to mention around this point in the guide that you should never be too precious with your idea. You may think it's the best idea in the world, but that doesn't mean it is - and there's nothing wrong with taking into consideration ideas from other people.

It doesn't make you any less of a writer to consider the views of those around you, whether they are friends and family or they're already in the industry. Remember that these people are looking out for you, and as long as you know what message you're pushing with your idea - everything else is fluid.

The best ideas are modified day to day in the development process, if something isn't working, feels forced or you know there's a better way of doing it (even if you don't exactly know how yet), put more time and work into it. Make your idea the best it can be.

When you think you're got your concept in place, then it's time to start building the action, characters, setting and secondary story threads around it. Many writers struggle with this part, as they've been so focused on the overall idea that they've forgotten about all the other aspects of the film.

It's a tricky part in the process and it's just as important as the idea itself - many even believe it's harder than creating the idea. It's important to highlight the importance of everything other than the idea, but it's hard to think of those other aspects in the same way.

Typically, when you tell somebody you're working on the film, it's the first thing people go to. "What's the idea?" or "What is it about?" are the first questions that seem to spring to mind, understandably. Why is the main story so important to people? It's probably the best draw, it's the thing that's going to sell the tickets, however, we're not just in the selling tickets business, we're in the entertainment industry. You can have the best idea in the world, but without strong characters and a well-thought out, well-developed setting, the idea could fall flat.

So, once you've thought of all that, guess what?

You're still not finished.

Now it's onto the outline. Now, people have so many ways of doing this, but it's probably easier to consider doing your outline as a single page document. Give brief accounts of the main plot points of your film, including all necessary characters and any other aspects you have thought of.

Each point on the outline should be pushing the story in some way. It shouldn't just be "Coffee scene" - it should be the detail, like what makes the coffee scene important, is it during that coffee scene that Sarah discovers her best friend has been sleeping with her husband? We need to know the important details for the whole story, not just random scene information.

Look over your outline as many times as you can and ask yourself the following questions;

- Is each point as strong as the last?

- Does this sound like it would make a good film?

- Could it be better?

If you're unhappy with any part of the process, always go back to it until you've got the result you believe in, after all, this is your baby. Now, it's onto the script.

The Script

The script is where things become simultaneously more exciting but also trickier. It's like a poison chalice, it's bitter-sweet, but in the end it's worth it.

The script is where the fine detail really counts, which is hard because you're likely only experienced in idea generation and possibly writing outlines by this point. The fine detail, especially when you're starting with a blank canvas, can be daunting.

With that said, the blank canvas should be just as exciting as it is nerve-racking. This is your opportunity to get everything out on paper, finally, even if you feel some kind of pressure to get it right first time.

Now, here's some important advice. You won't get it right first time, you'd have to be some kind of genius to get it right first time. Even the best writers and filmmakers of history have made significant changes to scripts/films during the production process - and even post-production process.

Reshoots are commonplace - where scenes are added and current scenes are adapted as they may not have worked as intended. Why? Because there can never be such thing as having too much pride in the film industry.

Nobody is perfect - it's probably the most important thing you can take from the film industry and apply to your life, no matter whether you stay in the independent filmmaking business after your first film, or you go on to do something else. We'll rarely get things right first time and it actually makes us stronger to admit when we could have done something better.

The good thing about the film industry is that even once your film has been completed, edited and distributed - you can still go back to it. An example of an independent filmmaker currently (at the date of publication) going through this process is Liam Regan, of My Bloody Banjo fame. Several years ago, Liam released My Blood Banjo in a limited capacity, with a DVD and BluRay release and a stint on Prime Video.

The film opened to a largely positive reception from critics and audiences, though due to the limited nature of its distribution, there wasn't much money to be made from it in the end.

Today, Liam Regan has gone back, added scenes (scenes he believes are stronger) and even gone as far as changing the ending, it was an alternative ending they shot at the time, but he's shown a willingness to admit an alternative version of the script may have been a stronger route to take.

Not only this, but by adapting the script at the time so that he had the ability to go back and do this, will also earn him some more money in distribution of the new cut and BluRay sales - getting his name back out there before he begins his new indie film project.

"Writing is all about rewriting: the best storytellers will constantly edit their outline as they go, adding, removing and shaping plot points and characters to achieve the best fit for their story. And remember: movie and TV scripts must adhere to a specific Industry standard format. A standard format across all screenplays ensure that the many people involved in making a movie have one, single vision for what should appear on screen. Professional screenwriters use specialized software to accomplish this—a program called Final Draft is the most popular" [4].

Strengthening the point, we have been making throughout this chapter, the above quote highlights the level of professionalism that is actually involved with the rewriting process. It's pretty much industry standard, so get used to it

In terms of software, as the quote above mentions, Final Draft is a very popular choice. CeltX is also used by many and has great reviews that you can find from a quick internet search. Which you choose to use is entirely up to you, there's no right or wrong answer. I know many that use CeltX because they believe it is more user-friendly and sets out clearly how to format your script. Tutorials on

YouTube can be very useful if you're struggling to get a grasp of it.

We will provide you with a list of items (with definitions) that make up the screenplay format, but most scriptwriting software will already help you out with this to a certain extent, often doing most of the formatting for you.

Scene Heading

Indent: Left: 0.0" Right: 0.0" Width: 6.0". A scene heading is a one-line description of the location and time of day of a scene, also known as a "slugline." It should always be in CAPS [5].

Example: EXT. WRITERS STORE - DAY reveals that the action takes place outside The Writers Store during the daytime.

Subheader

Indent: Left: 0.0" Right: 0.0" Width: 6.0". When a new scene heading is not necessary, but some distinction needs to be made in the action, you can use a subheader. But be sure to use these sparingly, as a script full of subheaders is generally frowned upon. A good example is when there are a series of quick cuts between two locations, you would use the term INTERCUT and the scene locations.

Action

Indent: Left: 0.0" Right: 0.0" Width: 6.0". The narrative description of the events of a scene, written in the present tense. Also less commonly known as direction, visual exposition, black stuff, description or scene direction. Remember - only things that can be seen and heard should be included in the action.

Character

Indent: Left: 2.0" Right: 0.0" Width: 4.0". When a character is introduced, his name should be capitalized within the action. For example: The door opens and in walks BRIAN, a thirty-something hipster with attitude to spare.

A character's name is CAPPED and always listed above his lines of dialogue. Minor characters may be listed without names, for example "TAXI DRIVER" or "CUSTOMER."

Dialogue

Indent: Left: 1.0" Right: 1.5" Width: 3.5". Lines of speech for each character. Dialogue format is used anytime a character is heard speaking, even for off-screen and voice-overs.

Parenthetical

Indent: Left: 1.5" Right: 2.0" Width: 2.5" A
parenthetical is direction for the character, that
is either attitude or action-oriented. With roots
in the
playwriting genre, today, parentheticals are
used very rarely, and only if absolutely
necessary. Why? Two reasons. First, if you
need to use a parenthetical to convey what's
going on with your dialogue, then it
probably just needs a good re-write. Second,
it's the director's job to instruct an actor on how
to deliver a line, and everyone knows not to
encroach on the director's turf!

Extension

Placed after the character's name, in
parentheses. An abbreviated technical note
placed after the character's name to indicate
how the voice will be heard

onscreen, for example, if the character is speaking as a voice-over, it would appear as HEATHER (V.O.).

Transition

Indent: Left: 4.0" Right: 0.0" Width: 2.0". Transitions are film editing instructions, and generally only appear in a shooting script. Transition verbiage includes:

- CUT TO:

- DISSOLVE TO:

- SMASH CUT:

- QUICK CUT:

- FADE TO:

As a spec script writer, you should avoid using a transition unless there is no other way to indicate a story element. For example, you might need to use DISSOLVE TO: to indicate that a large amount of time has passed.

Shot

Indent: Left: 0.0" Right: 0.0" Width: 6.0". A shot tells the reader the focal point within a scene has changed. Like a transition, there's rarely a time when a spec screenwriter should insert shot directions. Once again, that's the director's job. Examples of Shots:

- ANGLE ON --

- EXTREME CLOSE UP --

- PAN TO --

- JAKE'S POV

Pre-Production

The pre production process as a whole comprises of many elements that need to be completed before you can even think of pressing the record button. As we mentioned in the earlier chapters, there's nothing wrong with adapting what you already have when you get to the production process, or even the post production process - but you need something to get you going before you consider your fall backs.

The pre-production process comprises of the following aspects, typically; [6]

- Planning the film

- The premise

- The outline

- The treatment (a document full of research and supporting documents alongside the idea and outline to give somebody in the industry a clear idea of what you're looking to achieve with the project)

- Screenplay

- Storyboard - you don't need to be great at drawing, but storyboards help to give everybody a clear idea of where they should be at any given time. It also gives cast and crew members a visual insight into your brain.

- Character biographies - these are very important as they help you when writing the screenplay, giving you a point of reference for what your characters would and wouldn't do. You can judge them based on the biographies and make decisions based upon who they are as people. If the story for that character doesn't fit, then something needs to be changed.

- Breakdown sheets

- Production design

As mentioned, the pre-production refers to everything that happens before your video shoot can take place [7]. As a general rule nothing you see on screen is an accident, someone somewhere has planned it! In this case, probably you. It's probably your idea, your outline, your scene breakdowns, your storyboarding and you know where we're going with this.

Everything that would need organizing to make sure that when filming happens things can run like clockwork is all a part of the process.

The pre-production stage of a film is incredibly important, especially on larger shoots or if you know you will be filming on a tight deadline. In this case, it's more likely that you're working to a tight deadline, or you don't have much time planned with each of your locations. Time will be especially precious if you're working with predominantly extras and/or an unpaid cast. While they're usually happy to help, they don't want your film to become their life.

It is always important to remember that "people cost money", so if everyone is held up while a location or costume is sourced, or a script is still being written, that is not a cost-effective production!

Planning offers many advantages; [8]

- Planning saves time (your precious time, the crews' and talents' time,

and the costly equipment time). I can't say it enough, time is money. Repeat after me, "Time is money". Everybody, say it. Time is money.

- Planning makes the shoot go more smoothly - it goes without saying really that a clear plan is harder to deviate from than 'winging it' would be. A clear plan of action is good for the writer, director, cast and crew. You know exactly what you're wanting to achieve from the film, so go for it and get your plan started now.

- Planning makes for a more focused, better executed program - again, this is similar to the point above. Avoid distractions, keep focused and plan on a clear mind. The more focused your plan is, the better chance you have of executing it effectively.

- Planning keeps you sane, because it allows for you to anticipate, plan for, and deal with the problems that inevitably come up.

Throughout the pre-production process, it's always best to set goals and ask yourself a multitude questions before you're ready to

begin. These may include some of the
following;

- In terms of audience, you might be thinking "Who am I trying to reach?" or "What is the best way to reach this audience?"

- In terms of achieving goals - "Why am I making this production?" or "What is the purpose of the production?"

- "What do I want my audience to think, feel, or do as a result of seeing it?"

- "Is video the right tool for the job?"

The pre-production process in any form of filmmaking; whether it's the big budget Hollywood business or small independent filmmaking, is arguably the most important part of the three-step plan. It's where your idea can truly flourish and you get to see how it will hypothetically work on film, isn't that exciting?

Now, with all those aspects covered, you can move onto one of the most exciting parts of the process where you get to bring your vision to life. It's time to hold auditions - it's time to find the talent for your indie film. As you'll soon find out, this can go one of two ways, surprisingly successful… or very long, very tricky and bringing with it many problems for what comes next. Let's find out why…

The Talent

So, with everything else in place, it's time to find your talent. This can be one of the most exciting points for an independent filmmaker, as you've likely imagined what your protagonist, antagonist and secondary characters are like in your head - what they may look like and how they may speak. In the casting process, it all becomes reality - or at least that's the hope.

Finding the right talent for any film is difficult, particularly if you're an independent filmmaker where budgets are so often very tight, therefore the pay you can offer an actor isn't especially attractive. But, it's important to never lose hope that the perfect actor is out there - and willing to work for a price you can afford.

There are several ways you can do this, depending on your budget of course. Many independent filmmakers now turn to social media; using targeted hashtags on Twitter for actors looking for work, joining actor and extra groups on Facebook and even searching hashtags on Instagram. Social media is a powerhouse that is so often used in such an informal way that people often forget it has its professional benefits too.

For instance; I know a several extras/very small-time actors who created their own Facebook group specializing in zombie extra work specifically. Now, from searching things like 'zombie' and 'extra work' through Facebook's search function, many other actors and extras have now joined the group – also many small times producers, writers and directors. The community has had the ability to thrive just from being on Facebook. When producers and directors need extras for shoots coming up, or even last-minute jobs, they know they can count on the members of that group to step in and save the day.

This is a huge plus for using Facebook, as, even without the expense of paying for sponsored post coverage, you're search can still gain traction on the platform. However, it is worth noting that without the sponsored post coverage, you're going to need quite some time to build up your Facebook presence, giving people time to get to know who you are, what you're looking to do and whether or not they actually like the idea you're working on - surprisingly, most actors and extras do care about this. Another crucial piece of information is that sponsored posts can be very hit and miss, so try not to be too disappointed if you first one doesn't work out.

Furthermore, always keep an eye out for discounts and deals on sponsored post coverage, if you are looking to build that presence much quicker than you would do without paying for it. Both Facebook and Instagram offer linked sponsored post coverage, with the same post going out across the two platforms. With your first sponsored post, you'll often get a little bit of credit to get you started, so if you use it wisely, you can make your first sponsored post cost effective - just make sure the post you share is attracting the right people.

If you're an independent filmmaker (or aspiring to be one) and you live near a university, that's great. It's great for two reasons - you have drama students who are keen to take on fresh and exciting roles, usually for free (as it often helps with their coursework) and there's likely lots of graduates still living in the area.

These graduates could be trained in anything from drama to film production, so if you live near a university/ you're filming close to a university, then you are at a huge advantage over those who live out in the countryside away from civilization.

So, you're likely to find aspiring actors who will work for free, that's great… right? You certainly hope so. But, it's important not to approach the situation with rose tinted glasses - as those glasses may just shatter at the reality of what's to come.

In 2014, a friend of mine was producing a short film and turned to university students for his actors. To say he was disappointed with the turnout would be an understatement. Despite having only one crucial role (the only role in the film that required an actor with range), he struggled. Just one actor turned out to auditions and unfortunately, there was no time before filming to hold more auditions. The show had to go on and rather than focusing on what their one actor couldn't do, they tried to mould him, working tirelessly with him before the production process to ensure he understood the character completely and what was expected of him.

After asking my friend what went wrong and why only one person turned out for auditions, he told me it was the lack of social media activity. Well, not so much the activity itself, but rather the sporadic nature of his social media presence. It wasn't consistent, the message was able to be forgotten about - where he should have ensured through social media that each and every drama student knew about those auditions and more people would have turned out.

For guaranteed results, you're likely going to want to use websites like Star Now or something to the same effect. These websites allow for you to search for exactly the kind of actor you need. You can search by age, ratings, even hair colour, weight, height and many more categories.

Rather than putting posts out on social media and hoping for the best, by using websites like Star Now, you can arrange auditions with the people who appeal to you the most on paper, ensuring they definitely turn out on the day. This way, you're more likely to avoid the risk that comes with not having any concrete auditions in place - probably saving you a headache later down the line.

"So, where do I even hold auditions?" you might be asking, well, in this day and age, it's important to put the safety of yourself and your talent first. Meet in a safe location initially, then when you're more comfortable, work out what best for you both and go from there. The safety and comfort of everybody involved is very importance. But, with that said, try to make the audition process as fun and relaxed as possible.

Actors, despite oozing confidence, have the potential to freeze when they feel uncomfortable. You will likely find that if an actor really wants a gig, he/she will be more nervous because they feel as if they have more on the line - there's more to lose. So, do everything in your power to loosen them up and get them talking, laughing and joking around freely. After all, these are auditions - it is a chance for actors to express themselves, be creative with their performances, try out new approaches for the character and make an impression. They will only do this if they're invested in you as an independent filmmaker.

As mentioned earlier, as an independent filmmaker, you're likely to have more students/less experienced actors coming forward for auditions, do not let this bother you as it can be a positive too. Rather than coming into the process with a lot of preconceived ideas about what the industry is all about and how they should approach the character - you will likely have a higher chance at being able to mould them to exactly how you want the character to be - whilst still ensuring they are able to have a bit of creative input, encouraging them to make suggestions along the way.

The same goes for finding talent in terms of your independent filmmaking crew. Unless you're already part of a small production team, you'll likely be looking for small-time, possibly inexperienced camera operatives, lighting guys, gaffers, runners and make-up artists. Now, when you don't have much to give them in terms of a financial reward - you have to make sure they are fully behind the creative vision of the film instead and making sure they know they're a valued part in the creative machine that is your independent film.

Production

So, it's finally time to press the record button and get going on your film. You've already come so far but there's still a lot of hard work to do, particularly at this point.

You will notice at this part in the process that it all suddenly begins to feel real - because it is. Everything is in place; your script is ready, your script should have been read by your cast and crew, your idea has been realized, everybody has been briefed and knows what they need to do - and your locations are booked.

It's worth noting at this point that you will need a shared digital calendar in place for everybody involved in the process at this point - whether it's a runner in the crew or your leading actor in the role of the protagonist/antagonist. Particularly in the independent filmmaking business, where members of your cast and crew alike may be working other part time jobs and have other commitments they can't escape, you need to ensure everybody knows the plan.

This is usually a responsibility of the Producer, but depending on your crew size, this duty may fall with you. By having a calendar in place - people are much less likely to double-book themselves and have a point of reference to turn to when their mind wanders from the project and they begin to ask themselves questions. Questions like; "Is the shoot at 9am or 10am tomorrow?".

By having a calendar in place for everybody to access, it ensures the cast and crew alike avoid contacting the director over the upcoming plans - avoiding unnecessary conversation and freeing up the director/producer's time to further enhance his/hers creative vision for the project. Though, it's important to point out that both the director and producer, no matter how big or small the project is, probably should be contactable for questions on the creative side of things - able to answer questions in order to further guide them in the journey to fully understanding the project and its aims.

"The production stage is where the rubber hits the road. The Writer, Director, Producer, and countless other creative minds finally see their ideas captured on film, one day at a time. Production is usually the shortest of the five phases, even though it is paramount to the film and where most of the budget is allotted. Production is the busiest time, with the crew swelling to hundreds and the days becoming longer in order to be as efficient as possible with all the gear and locations on hire" [9].

Though the above may not be entirely accurate for a smaller, independent project, it's important to highlight the importance of what the production phase means for the creative minds involved in the project. As mentioned in the above quotation, this is the first instance where the creative minds of the project will see their ideas captured on screen - they're finally able to feel valued - as their ideas make it to the screen.

It's also worth noting that production may not be the shortest phase of the project, this is all dependent on the project, the cast and the crew involved. The script can be an important factor in this; for instance, if your film includes locations that require bright, summery weather but snowy winters too, your filming schedule may need to be split in two, which can certainly make filming difficult!

"The crew works extremely hard during this period, with shooting hours each day ranging up to sixteen hours. Projects run to strict schedules with cast only contracted for a certain time frame, so the crew is crucial in squeezing out every bit of energy to see the project successfully completed on time" [9].

What To Expect

There are many things you should prepare yourself for when it comes to reaching the production process. As such an important phase in the independent filmmaking process, there are obviously many positive and negative things to watch out for.

A good independent filmmaker will recognize everything they should look forward to and acknowledge the areas where things may go wrong, and is therefore able to put other arrangements in place to minimize risk.

Questions, So Many Questions

As an independent filmmaker, whether you're taking the role of the producer, director or writer (or all three), expect questions from all directions. Whether it's questions on character choices and development from your leading man or leading lady, questions on the script or maybe even deviating from what is on the page.

It is worth considering that a talented actor, whether they are experienced or not, will be able to fully digest the character they are about to play, who they are, their motivations and their story. A talented actor should therefore know the character almost as well as you do, and may be able to bring new ideas to the table. As we mentioned earlier in the book, approach this with the openness it deserves - as nobody is perfect and they may even have some great ideas that you can take on board.

The last thing you want to do when you are presented with ideas from your talent is to shut them down entirely. Even if the idea is one that you would never even consider using, always explain your reasoning, do not discourage them from making further suggestions and use it as an opportunity to further explain the character they are playing. There's always a chance that there's an aspect of that character's personality traits that they haven't considered when they thought of their suggestion.

Use each and every question as an opportunity for as many people as possible to grow within the independent filmmaking process. Rather than allowing people to feel discouraged, under-appreciated and forgotten about, always encourage the idea that you're open to hearing from cast and crew alike - no matter what phase of the process you're in. You can always go back and make changes to strengthen your film - so take every opportunity that is brought to you that you think might work.

You May Have A Few Divas

Though this is much less likely on the set of an indie film, it's still possible that if you're dealing with inexperienced actors, particularly university drama students (ranging between around 18-25), that you just might encounter this.

We're not saying it's entirely an age thing or even a lack of experience in the business, as divas exist in many forms, but you may be more likely to find them when you're dealing with students. It seems to be that university students, along with the complete opposite end of the spectrum (big time Hollywood actors) are known for this. With all that said, the best independent filmmakers are always equipped with the tools they need in order to deal with this type of person effectively.

"So, what should I expect from a diva?" you may be asking. Well, that is potentially a very long list, but with our help and advice, there's no need to worry!

Particularly with university students, you need to consider that even with a shared calendar in place, there's still the potential for them to not show up on time, or even at all. Some university students will prioritize drinking and partying over the course they have chosen to study and the opportunities given to them. With that said, you cannot go into the process expecting this from any drama students you cast in your roles, as this is unfair. The best you can do is have procedures in place to deal with this. If an actor is late for a shoot, speak to them privately and discuss`with them the reasons why they were late.

You cannot go into this private conversation expecting that they were late because they were out partying the previous night, as for all you know, they may have been dealing with an important personal issue. They may have been late because a family member was rushed to

hospital - there could be many reasons outside
of the stereotype of a student.

If they appear intoxicated or hungover and you
have a strong suspicion that they were drinking
the previous night, you need to deal with the
situation in a professional manner - but as this
is the independent filmmaking process - you
can handle it a little differently than the big time
Hollywood film industry.

Though your time is still very thinly spread,
your team is likely to be much smaller than that
of a big budget Hollywood film, therefore you
have a greater opportunity to give your actors
the attention they deserve. If an actor arrives in
a state of intoxication, find out the reasons why
they thought that was acceptable, give them a
warning and always make sure they know how
this has affected the production process.

It's crucial that they know just how significant their actions have been and the effect they've had on your schedule. By understanding the severity of their actions, they can adapt their working attitude for future shoots - and hopefully prove to you that they are willing to take the production of this film serious.

Be firm but fair - but make sure they know there's no time for them to mess you around. At the end of the day, as harsh as it sounds, they are replaceable. If it helps you to feel more comfortable about the possibility of your chosen actors being divas, think of this in the casting process. Consider adding questions in for after the auditions where you get to know them more as a person, rather than just an actor. That way, you can see just how serious they are about your creative vision and how passionate they are about their craft.

Sticky Situations

When it comes to the production process, the chance that something will go wrong is disturbingly high. That's why, as an independent filmmaker, you need to consider every possibility.

The best independent filmmakers will understand and acknowledge every possibility, so they know exactly how to manage it if it becomes a problem during the process. This takes skill, confidence, motivation and careful planning. These are all skills you should have been developing up to this point in the process anyway.

"So, what sticky situations may I find myself in?" you may be asking. The list could go on forever really, and no two independent films are the same, a situation that may arise for you, another independent filmmaker may never even experience throughout their entire career. There's no way of knowing exactly what will happen before it does, so, the best you can do is plan for what might.

Disagreements

When it comes to creativity, you're likely to disagree with somebody on something - and if this disagreement arises on location during a shoot, it's even more difficult to deal with.

If an actor loves and cherishes their character as much as you do, expect that passion to shine through in the most extreme ways; good and bad. There's no way of really telling how this might happen but if you go into the production process understanding that this may very well happen, you can try and set limitations for how critical it can be.

Christian Bale famously disagreed with Shaun Hurlbut, the Director of Photography on the set of Terminator Salvation. The rant, which was recorded and distributed on many online platforms showed Christian Bale losing his temper in front of the crew. Now, we're not saying this will happen to you, it's unlikely that you will find someone with the passion Christian Bale has for his craft, or even the confidence to speak out in such a brash way.

We're not saying you're safe in this department either though, we're just saying, be prepared for it. Being able to diffuse a situation is beneficial for the independent filmmaking process but also life outside of your independent filmmaking career. No matter what job you're in, you're going to experience an angry customer, client or colleague at some point, so knowing how to deal with their grievance is the first step in rectifying the situation and setting their mind at peace.

The cast and crew will appreciate this too, not only the person you have the disagreement with, but also the rest of your team. Nobody, including yourself and the person you're dealing with, wish to argue over creative differences when there's still so much left to shoot. So, do your best to calm them down, explain your thought process behind your decision and ensure they are on board with what you're asking from them. Make them feel comfortable, make them feel cherished, that way, you should be fine.

Romances

Again, much less likely to be an issue on an independent film, but when you have a small cast and crew, the atmosphere is a lot more 'up close and personal', meaning there's more time to get to know everybody. Therefore, there's a possibility for romance to flourish - and we all know what that means; there's the possibility for fallout…

When a relationship ends, whether it was short and sweet or long and drawn out, it can unfortunately turn sour very quickly. Let's say your leading man and leading lady get together off-screen and split before you've finished filming, it could potentially be very tricky to manage. This is especially possible if these actors do not have much previous acting experience. Not understanding how to professionally manage an off-screen split can be dangerous for both the independent filmmaker and the actor - and can spell disaster for the film.

If there needs to be chemistry on screen between your leading man and leading lady, and they have just officially split off-screen, it can be tricky to act like that spark is still there, with both actors having to fight through all the negativity to get where you need them to be emotionally.

Unfortunately, there's not much you can do in this situation to limit to repercussions. All you can do is be there for your cast and crew and guide them where needed to ensure the finished product is the best it can be. You cannot outright stop your cast and crew from getting together off-screen, but you can manage how they feel if it turns sour. Ensure they know that you're there for them emotionally and on a professional level so that they know you're behind them every step of the way.

By doing that, you're well on your way to becoming a successful independent filmmaker who effectively knows how to manage people and the sticky situation of romance, wait… that sounds wrong.

I Quit!

The words no filmmaker wants to hear, independent or not. Whether it's a disgruntled member of the crew or an actor who's just not getting it, the words 'I quit' spell headaches for everybody involved in your film - particularly if you've already shot a significant chunk of it.

It goes without saying that it's of top importance that you keep your cast and crew as happy as they can possibly be, ensuring they feel respected, valued and trusted throughout the entire process. Always be positive with them, ensuring all those criteria are met and you shouldn't go far wrong. Nobody wants to hear those words, so do everything in your power to prevent it.

It's like they say, prevention is cheaper than the cure. This couldn't be any more accurate than when applied to this situation.

"So, what do I do if somebody does quit?" you may be asking yourself. Firstly, speak to them privately if you are able to. Take them out of the chaotic atmosphere of a shoot where everybody may be feeling the pressure and stress of their daily duties and speak to them in a calm, relaxed environment.

Find out exactly what it is that is making them unhappy and see if there's anything you can do to make it right. No member of any cast and crew wants to get halfway through a film and quit, only to be replaced - they've invested time in this project too, so it's likely that they have a set of 'demands'. Do everything in your power to ensure these demands are met, providing they are reasonable and do not negatively impact your creative vision.

With the ability to diffuse a situation and prevent hearing those words, you won't go far wrong. But, in the unlikely event you do hear the words from a disgruntled cast/crew member, do your best to make it right. That's all you can do, but if they're certain they're leaving, it's just an unfortunate situation you need to deal with. So, always bear in mind having a plan in place in case of emergency.

Camera

As an independent filmmaker, you may have had direct experience with a camera before, but it's just as likely that you haven't. As the independent filmmaker, you may have just stuck to the creative process - whether it's writing, directing and producing. So, when it comes to the technical side of things, you may find yourself a little stuck.

But, not to worry, as you can refer to your ultimate guide for, well, guidance… In this chapter, we would like you to leave it believing that the camera work is just as important in the creative process as everything you have done up until now. This is where whoever is in the role of the director can really flourish, allowing their style to compliment the script and performances to create something truly magical.

"Cinematography is the art of visual storytelling. Anyone can set a camera on a

tripod and hit record, but the artistry of cinematography comes in controlling what the viewer sees (or doesn't see) and how the image is presented. Film is a visual medium, and the best-shot films are ones where you can tell what's going on without hearing any of the dialogue" [10].

As you can see from the above quotation, with camera work comes the art of cinematography. This is a director's chance to put his/her stamp on the film and make it his/her own - all whilst ensuring he/she maintains the integrity of the film and ensuring the message remains strong. A strong film will tell you visually how to feel, with dialogue helping to compliment it. A strong film does not rely on purely dialogue to drive the story, therefore the cinematography is just as important as any other aspect.

It's worth noting that even if your demographic just watches the trailer for your film, they need to be wowed visually or they are unlikely to be interested. People like to watch things but find listening to be a much harder skill to maintain, therefore, capture the attention with strong and stunning visuals and you'll keep them for the story and dialogue. Create something that encapsulates all aspects of what defines a strong film, always keeping in mind the cinematography.

"With some basic knowledge of composition and scene construction, you can plan scenes using this visual language. Learn how different shots work together to form a clear, cohesive narrative and how to compose each shot in a way that is visually pleasing for the viewer. Understanding these simple rules will help

make your films more thrilling and engaging"
[10].

That is what it's all about, visually pleasing the
audience in order to keep them for the story,
dialogue and characters. You can have the
most well-written, carefully articulated dialogue,
but without the cinematography to back it up, it
may just fall flat. So, it's important to avoid
losing any aspect of your film, especially the
very good parts. Creating a well-rounded film
that considers all aspects of the process and
makes them the best they can be will ensure
your film has the highest possible chance for
success.

The Rule of Thirds

This is a technique that involves dividing the
camera frame up into a 3x3 grid. This splits
your camera up into nine equally sized boxes.

"Our natural impulse is to put our subject dead center, but a centered subject will look like they're caught in a spotlight, and by dropping them in the center of the frame, it gives them nowhere to go. Instead, by positioning your action in any of the four vertices where those nine boxes meet, you create a balance in your composition that feels more natural" [10].

Try out new things with the Rule of Thirds, even ignore it completely if you wish to really make an impact. It's all about your creative vision and the impression you want to give your audience. If you're going for something off-kilter and want your piece to really reflect that, play around with the Rule of Thirds and find something that best suits your style.

Be Unique

We have all seen a film or a TV series where a character does something completely mundane, like a daily chore and we have no idea why we had to see it. So, if you're going to include scenes like this, find a different way of shooting it, make it look way more interesting than it really is and try and convey a message visually that makes the audience consider why we're seeing what we're seeing.

If you're going to do this, make sure the answer isn't laid out for them in its entirety but make it like a puzzle - because it will certainly be rewarding for them if they work it out.

It goes without saying that the cinematography is an opportunity for a director to make his mark on the script, so do it in the most unique way that rings true with the source material. Don't follow the crowd and you're surely onto a winner.

Types of Shots

"Your camera is a surrogate for your audience. The way it interacts with the scene dictates the way your audience feels they are interacting with the scene. How do you want your audience to feel watching a scene? Do you want them to feel disoriented? Detached? Should the story feel serene, off-balance, or static? Do you focus on sweeping grandeur or small details? Different shots convey different tones to a scene; answering these questions first will help decide what types of shots to use" [10].

Now, we're going to take a lot at various types of shots and the impression they can have on your audience. We hope that in doing so, this will guide you to make the right choices that best support the source material you're working with.

Extreme Long Shot

You can probably guess what you might need an extreme long shot for. Correct, it's for subjects that are typically HUGE in size and scale. Let's say you have a huge tower and you have just one average sized man climbing that tower, you may wish to use an extreme long shot. This can show the insignificance of the character, being so small in comparison to the 'beast' he/she is trying to 'defeat'. It also goes a long way in giving the impression that your subject is majestic in size and scale - a thing of beauty.

Long Shot

Often used to reflect the emotion distance between the characters on set. In a way, it makes viewers a casual bystander, somewhat aloof to what's happening. For instance; say your leading man and leading lady are an onscreen couple and they are arguing, the details of their argument are lost and only the explosive parts catch our attention. Something is happening, but we can't be sure what it is. It all adds to the intrigue.

Medium Shot

This kind of shot feels more personal, it's just what you would expect to actually see when you would be having a casual conversation with somebody in real life - therefore it also feels more natural than the others. It allows us to engage with the characters on a personal level, allowing to feel part of it - even though you know you aren't really. It's almost camera-trickery, but you're in on the act and you're still fooled! It's actually very clever and if it is used correctly, it goes a long way in helping the audience to fully engage with and appreciate your characters. This way, the audience will further appreciate and invest in the story you are trying to tell.

What more could you ask for? The medium shot, if used correctly and only where necessary and where it complements the scene, can be very powerful.

Close Up

This kind of shot is more intimate than using a medium shot, when used correctly and effectively. It allows you to hone in on the facial expressions and emotions that the character is conveying. It's direct, it's personal and more importantly, when used right, it really feels real.

It's worth highlighting that by using close-ups, you do lose much of the setting you've chosen to use - but this is replaced with a more intimate shot that can potentially be much more impactful. Like we said, it all depends on the scene, you just need to find what works for your story, going scene by scene.

Extreme Close Up

For amplifying emotional intensity, the extreme close-up puts the camera right in the actor's face, making even their smallest emotional cues huge - and raises the intensity of the problems behind them. This works for objects too: the ticking hands of a clock, a bullet shell hitting the floor, the blinking cursor of a computer terminal. What the extreme close up lacks in context, it makes up for it by taking a small event and making it enormous.

Lighting

From even doing a quick internet search, you will find so many sources that can assist you with lighting techniques - and there are lots of them out there. In this guide, we'll focus on the techniques that are likely to best suit an independent film, whilst encouraging you to go out and learn more about lighting. Again, it's a key part of the creative process and can really make your audience engage with the piece.

"Every cinematographer is an artist who makes creative decisions on how to guide the viewer's eye within the frame using lighting equipment. Their applications are broad, but their creative interpretation is what makes their lighting cinematic (or not)" [11].

Basic Lighting: The Three Point Lighting Set Up

As it says on the tin, this is the most basic lighting technique in film - there's no arguing it as it's right there for all to see. It involves lighting your subject from three directions to create shape and set them apart from their background [11].

The most basic lighting in film is the three-point lighting setup. Lighting from three directions shapes your subject and sets them apart from their background.

Key Light: The key light is the light that registers most prominently in your frame.

Fill Lights: Quite simply, fill lights fill in the shadows of your frame.

Back Light: The back light gives an edge light to the rear portion of your subject. Often, the back light shoots down from a higher angle.

Soft Film Lighting

Hard or soft lighting can impact heavily on how a scene feels emotionally. This is something that most filmmakers will consider when making decisions on lighting, as it subliminally conveys a message, whether it's intended or not.

The hardness or softness of light concerns how large a light source is, and how it affects shadows on your subject.

High Key Light: This is an effect created by heightening the key light and using fill lights generously. This keeps the lighting bright and balanced in your frame, creating almost no shadow. This balances the lighting from object to object in your frame -- which is known as your lighting ratio.

Diffused Overhead Lighting: You can soften a light source with diffusion materials like gels or Chinese lanterns to reduce shadows. This is great for conversation close-ups.

Hard Film Lighting

Kicker Light with Soft Fill: The back light is able to hit the side of your subject's face. It can create an angelic rim of light, while a very soft fill light keeps the face gently illuminated.

Low Key Light: This technique refers to minimizing, or eliminating the fill light for your shot so that it is intentionally shadowy. This can create dramatic, suspicious, or even scary effects.

When making your choice with lighting techniques, it's always best to consider the following questions before making your final decision. These questions should guide you so you can make a fully formed argument in your reasoning.

- Which props and scene elements should be emphasized?

- Whose perspective are we witnessing the scene through?

- How much light should they be able to see at that given moment?

- How should the characters differ from one another in each frame?

- Which emotions are being expressed through harshness of light, or color?

By considering all the above questions - and any more you can think of, you will be well on your way to becoming a lighting expert who can share his knowledge with the rest of the cast and crew.

Sound

"Sound refers to everything we hear in a movie — words, sound effects, and music. Sound is used in film to heighten a mood, provide us with information about the location of a scene, advance the plot, and tell us about the characters in the story" [12].

Some of our favorite films have reached that level of favoritism because they have effectively, and more importantly, memorably used sound. Most recently, the film *Hereditary*, written and directed by Ari Aster, used sound effectively to really keep the attention of the audience.

I remember watching the trailer for the film at the movie theatre and hearing as the daughter in the film (played by Milly Shapiro) made this tongue clicking sound. The sound resonated with me, it was different and it was in a horror film, it just felt plain creepy. It made me feel uneasy because it was something I wasn't used to and it added to the creepy atmosphere portrayed in the trailer. I just knew, purely from that sound alone, that I had to see the film when it came out. Sure enough, a few weeks later when it arrived in movie theatres, I was there.

That alone shows just how effective sound can be when used correctly, you can make an audience member really feel something. Whether you want them to feel uneasy or upbeat and cheery - there's a sound for it. It's just all about finding what works for you, your film and the message your film is all about.

"There are two categories of sound in film; diegetic and non-diegetic. Diegetic sound refers to all those audio elements that come from sources inside the world we see on the screen, including dialogue, doors slamming, footsteps, etc. Non-diegetic Sound refers to all those audio elements that come from outside of the fictional world we see on screen, including the musical score and sound effects like the screeches in the shower scene in Psycho" [12].

No sound is stronger than another. It may seem odd to be saying that, but it's all about the way it is used. For instance; would the tongue click from *Hereditary* have worked in Ari Aster's more recent film *Midsommar*? Maybe, but there's no way to tell for sure. All we do know is that the tongue clicks really worked for the film it belonged to. Much like groaning/pleasure sounds from the odd sex ritual worked in *Midsommar*. They work because they make us feel uneasy - and the ideas those films are based around have been created to make us feel uneasy. They go against the grain in order to tell a different kind of story, one that we may never have heard otherwise. These sounds, in both of Ari Aster's films, made an impression - and I'll always remember them.

"Sound effects can be used to add mood or atmosphere to a film by creating a

soundscape that accents or adds another layer of meaning to the images on the screen. Pitch, tempo, and volume may be altered to indicate how the filmmaker expects the audience to respond to a given noise" [12].

"So, how do I effectively use sound in my film?" you may be asking yourself. There's no right or wrong answer, it's just all about finding what works for your film, its tone and the impression you want to give the audience. For instance; using a creepy tongue click in a film like

American Pie probably would have been a bit jarring. Find what suits all the other aspects of your film.

Remember, your decisions always have to compliment the rest of your independent film recipe, otherwise you'll spoil the final product.

Always Have a Plan B

Regardless of which part of the production phase you're thinking about, you need a 'Plan B' for everything. Now, this can be tricky as it's almost like planning a second film where the plans may never even get used.

As we mentioned earlier in the book, it's important to consider every situation so that you're ready for when/if disaster strikes and you can effectively manage and deal with the situation.

In this chapter, we'll simply reiterate some of the most important aspects of the production process that you should have a 'Plan B' in place for;

Cast and Crew Quitting

Though it's unlikely you will ever experience this during the production process, it's still crucial to know what to do in case of emergency. Remember, they may not be quitting because of on-set disagreements, they may be quitting because of a bereavement or long-term illness.

This is why it is crucial to consider this back in the casting process. Cast your favorite actor but also keep in mind a 'second choice' for each role. As harsh as it sounds to call them

that, you may just need them. This way, it
saves going back and holding further auditions.

This is considerably harder when it comes to a
member of the crew leaving. But, luckily,
there's a lot of people who are invested in the
film industry who are also unfortunately (for
them) out of work. These people can be found
on various freelancing websites, such as
Craigslist, Star Now, Facebook and many more.
These people are actively seeking work,
whether it's for financial benefit or simply just to
get their name out there, so always check
these websites before you go into panic mode.

Scenes Just Not Working

If a scene isn't gelling the way you wanted it,
don't dwell on it. Go back to the drawing board
(or should we say computer?) and either
rewrite it or write a new scene entirely. It's
probably worth noting that you should write

more scenes than you need, filming more just in case you need to make any significant changes to your edits later down the line. If you're struggling, let actors have their say on how the scene should be done. Never hold onto your pride - be confident in asking for help, the best filmmakers consider the opinions of everybody around them, not just their own.

Punctuality

This is probably the most likely aspect of the production process that you will need a 'Plan B' in place for, as when you're dealing with so many cast and crew members, somebody is bound to be late. Always have another plan in place in case you can't film things in the order you initially wanted to, because a crucial member of the cast/crew hasn't arrived yet. Film what you can without compromising on the quality and be efficient with your time.

Post Production

You've made it, young grasshopper. At this point, you've completed two hugely important phases in the independent filmmaking process. The pre-production elements you'd worked so hard on finally paid off and now you've finished filming. So, what comes next?

"Post Production includes editing, but it is much more than that. Post begins with the script and continues in the Pre-Production phase with the planning, scheduling and budgeting the of finishing processes. During

Production the Editor is syncing dailies and assembling a rough cut for the Director to view as the shooting progresses. Finally, there is the sound design, scoring, titles, visual effects, mix, printing and delivery that comprise the finishing process" [13].

There are arguably thirteen steps involved with the post-production process, as described by Raindance [14]. Here, we will briefly outline them before going further in-depth in order to guide you as you reach the end of your independent filmmaking journey.

The 13 Steps of Post-Production

1. Choose an Editing Format: There are two ways of doing post-production. One is the old way — the film way. Shoot film and edit, or splice film on film editing equipment. There are few filmmakers who edit this way today.

The second is the digital way. Two is the new way — the electronic way. Get all your film digitized (if shot on film you will need them telecined, or scanned to a digital format).   The steps are pretty much the same in either format.

2. Hire A Picture Editor: Your cinematographer is probably a good person to ask for recommendations for an editor. An editor's job is to create an Edit Decision List (EDL). The editor will read your script and look at the rushes, and from this information, cut the film according to their opinion of what makes the story better. Given this huge creative responsibility, I always like to get an editor well before the project goes into production. A good editor will advise on the types of shots they will need, and advise on tricky post-production issues before the film starts.

The normal schedule for editing a feature is 8 – 10 weeks. During this time, your editor will create different drafts of your film. The first is called the Rough Cut, and last is the Answer Print. There are two conclusions to an edit: the first when you are happy with the visual images (locking picture) and the second when you are happy with the sound (sound lock).

3. Hire A Sound Editor: Now, about two months later, the picture film is tight but you need to enhance the look with sound. Thus, hire a sound editor and an assistant for five to six weeks to (a) cut dialogue tracks, (b) re-create sound effects, and (c) get cue sheets ready for simplifying Step 7, The Mix.

4. Do ADR: This stands for Automatic Dialogue Replacement. What it actually is, is a large hollow room with a projector that projects your most recent picture draft from Step 2 and has the actors come back and lip sync and loop dialogue that wasn't sharp and clear.

5. Do Foley: Go to a room that looks like (or could very well be) the ADR room and this time, without actors, have sound people called Foley Artists – or sometimes 'walkers' – put the noise of footsteps and certain other sound effects into your film.

6. Secure Music: First, for your musical score here's what not to do. Don't use any popular old song that you haven't purchased the rights to. Don't use any pre-cleared CD-ROM music because it won't be good enough quality. What you should do is simply this: hire a musician with his or her own studio to compose brand new original songs and tunes that you have the rights to. Alternatively, as this is probably still out of reach for an independent filmmaker, simply find license free music that you can use - but make sure it comes with the correct permissions to use it for commercial purposes. This is crucial.

7. Do Re-recording/Mix: Now that you have 20-40 tracks of sound (dialogue, ADR, Foley, music) you must layer them on top of each other to artificially create a feeling of sound with depth. This is called the re-recording session or the Mix.

8. Get an M&E: Somewhere in the not-too-distant future you will be selling the rights to your film to foreign nations. The distributor/buyer in that nation wants a sound track without English dialogue so they can dub the dialogue. Thus the M&E stands for only Music and Effects.

In the movie I just made, we waited until we had a sale where they demanded an M&E track – in our case to Latin America. Then we used part of the proceeds to pay for it.

9. Get Your Titles: Your editing is now done. Now what is left is to get the final pieces needed for the answer print. The first three pieces to get are your six-to-eight Opening Title Cards and then the Rear Title Crawl. These title files are then added to the master track.

10. Get a DCP: In order to deliver the film, you will need to create a Digital Cinema Package – a hard drive which contains the final copy of your film encoded so it can play in cinemas.

11. Get a Dialogue Script: In order for foreign territories to dub or subtitle your film you will need to create a dialogue script which has the precise time code for each piece of dialogue so the subtitler or dubbing artist knows exactly where to place their dialogue. This is much less likely to be needed for an independent film unless you're willing (and it's mainstream enough) to take it internationally.

12. Get a Campaign Image: A picture says a thousand words. Your campaign image is likely the first thing a prospective distributor or festival programmer will see of your film. The image (with titles and credits) should let the viewer know exactly what your film is about.

13. **Get a Trailer:** Create a 90-120 second trailer that conveys the mood and atmosphere of your movie. Often programming and distribution decisions will be based on the strength of your trailer. This can be one of the most exciting parts of the post-production process, as you can finally tease your family, friends and demographic with the film they've all been waiting to see, especially after they've heard you talking about it for so long.

It's worth noting that not all these steps may apply to your film, they are simply detailed by Raindance as a guide for how to approach the post production phase. We'll be focusing on the crucial steps going forward. So, enjoy, and like all other aspects of this book, make the most of it, as we're here to help you throughout the entire process.

Editing

Editing your film can often feel even more daunting than the planning and actual production was. It's the part of the post production phase where your film literally and metaphorically comes together. You're able to craft the footage you have into something magical and majestic.

With this, comes the chance for further creativity, as you look for ways to enhance what you've got on film.

"When individual shots are edited together, filmmakers have a number of editing techniques at their disposal. The importance of these techniques is that they often happen so quickly that we don't notice them at all. Becoming aware of where these techniques are used in movies is important in order to understand the constructed nature of all moving images" [15].

Some of the most common editing techniques include; [15]

Simple Cuts: which are breaks from one shot to the next. Cuts carry the continuity of action forward in a straightforward manner, from action to action or place to place.

Jump Cuts: which are confusing cuts from one shot to the next that do not follow the obvious rules of cause and effect. These cuts are usually used to disrupt the audience's attention in order to create shock.

Fade-downs: These edits are able to show the screen fade from an image to a black screen.

Fade-ups: These show the screen fade from black to an image. Both fade-ups

and fade-downs are used to suggest the passage of time and generally work to give the audience a chance to take a breath in preparation for the next scene.

Dissolves: These show one image slowly disappear as a new image is

introduced. Dissolves are used to indicate the end of one event and the beginning of a new event or scene.

Wipes: These show one part of the screen literally wipe over the rest of the screen. One image disappears as it is replaced by a new image. This kind of edit is not often seen in movies, largely because it looks comic-bookish. For this very reason, wipes were used throughout Star Wars as it gives the impression from the get-go that it is like a comic book, focusing heavily on fantasy and science fiction elements - much like a Marvel comic would.

Editing techniques can leave a lasting impression on your audience, and much like every other aspect of the independent film process - decisions need to be made based on the requirements of your film.

Your decisions cannot be made because 'it works for me', it needs to be something your demographic would like to see that doesn't compromise the quality of the film and holds the integrity of the message you are trying to convey. For instance, if you're making a period drama piece - you probably wouldn't want to implement wipes in the editing process, as this could feel jarring for the audience.

Distribution

You finally have your finished independent film. Congratulations, over the course of this guide, you've achieved so much and it's finally paid off. Your finished project is something that you can be proud of and that your friends, family and demographic will hopefully love.

But, what do you do with your film then? Well, there's various avenues to consider when it comes to distributing your independent film.

"At script stage filmmakers should have already asked themselves: who is the audience and how best to reach them? Now it's important to ask again, and to be objective" [16].

- What type of film is this and what have I achieved in making it? Has this film been created for your personal pleasure? Has it been a hobby or the start of your filmmaking career? Is your work going to be of genuine interest to people?

  - Who is the audience for your film?

  - What separates your film from others in the same genre? What are the unique selling points for your audience?

- Would I pay to see this film?

- Would I be disappointed if I had paid to see this film?

- Could people be disappointed by paying to see this film?

- Is this film more suited to being an unexpected addition to a film festival, or does it deserve its screen time in movie theatres?

"The classic route of a film to its audience is as follows. The producer secures the services of a sales agent who represents the film at major festivals and markets to different international distributors and television companies. Having shown at festivals, the film is distributed to cinemas, then non-theatrical exhibitors" [16].

Of course, today, things are much different. With the inclusion of online streaming platforms, it's actually much easier today to have your finished film distributed than it would have been even ten years ago.

Netflix are known for buying up cheap properties in order to add them to their vast library of low-budget films from lesser known producers and directors, often paying exactly what it cost the independent filmmaker or small-scale studio to make it. That way, the studio/filmmaker gain the exposure they need, getting their name and film out there for the masses to watch (with millions of subscribers just waiting for new content). Additionally, the money from selling the distribution rights to the film mean that the filmmaker can move onto his/her next project.

It's like Walt Disney said "We don't make movies to make money, we make money to make more movies". Though, you should hope that the more you're getting your name and films out there, the better chance you have of making a bit more money from it.

Whichever route you decide to take, you're probably going to need to get yourself a sales agent. Sales agents are often referred to as 'distributors' but rarely handle theatrical releasing, so always bare that in mind.

Different sales agents deal with different genres, lengths and styles of film (but ultimately, each will take on what they know they can sell, like we mentioned before, the business is unfortunately all about money). Sales agents commonly have long-standing, trusted relationships with a network of buyers to whom they represent rights at festivals and markets.

What Next?

So, you've distributed your film, the reviews are
rolling in (whether they're from friends or family
members, cinema audiences or festival
audiences) and now you're unsure of what to
do next.

Well, that all depends on what your intentions
were for making the first film - and what your
bank balance is looking like now. If your

intentions with your first film were to make a lot of money, and that hasn't quite worked out, then you may want to quit now - as the independent filmmaking journey can be a very long and very difficult one, with many more tribulations over triumphs.

If you're in this for the long haul, keep at it. Move onto your next project, taking into consideration everything you have learned in this guide and using the practical experience from your first stint to become an even better filmmaker the second time around.

It's highly likely that you encountered many bumps along the road during the pre-production, production and post-production phases of your first film, so how would you approach those speed bumps the second time around? By understanding the problems, you faced the first time around and how you dealt with them, you can now use that information and analyse how it went - and what you would do differently if that same situation manifested itself in any films you make in the future.

With practice, doesn't come perfect, but comes knowledge and wisdom that will help to grow for future projects. You will notice that the more you practice filmmaking, the more confidence you develop, the more risks you are willing to take and the greater your chance for success will be.

Furthermore, you can fully develop your creative 'voice', whether it's as a producer, director or writer, you can be constantly working on your 'stamp' - recognizable traits that your audience can attach to your name, the same way that people attach gratuitous violence to Tarantino and his films. By continuing to make films, you are giving yourself more time to find your niche, find the thing that makes people go "this is definitely a [INSERT YOUR SURNAME HERE] film" without even reading up about it before their viewing.

You should be excited about your filmmaking future, because we certainly are.

All The Best

And now all that's left to say is our final farewell. Whether you've finished your first film, using this guide as a step-by-step along your journey or you've read it all before you even begin, we wish you all the best in everything you do.

A filmmaker's job is never really over, as even once your final film is done, distributed and dissected, it will likely remain with you and many others for the rest of your lives. Whether you wish to escape it or not, people will always have questions for you about your films and your career in particular.

See, people generally find the film industry absolutely fascinating, so you really won't ever escape what it's like to be a filmmaker once you've put even one film out there. Making your first film really is life-changing; it's exciting, thrilling, motivating and inspiring - hopefully pushing you into deciding to continue for a second film and many more after that.

Now you're at this point in the guide, whether you've made your first film or you're just about to, you'll realize just how difficult the process is, despite it being a bucket load of fun too. There are so many aspects to consider and as you've learnt, no single aspect of the independent filmmaking process is more important than another. All aspects of the process work together, like cogs in a well-oiled machine - and you should be the oil. You should have, or should be about to ensure all the parts are functioning together for the greater good.

A competent filmmaker will have the necessary skills to ensure everything within each phase of the independent filmmaking process is running like clockwork. Combining time management skills, leadership skills and the ability to work in a team to create the ultimate film cast and crew - ready for anything that might come their way.

We hope that throughout this guide, you have taken on board each and every piece of advice we have to offer you. No two filmmakers are the same, we understand that, but by following our guide, you do stand yourself in good stance for the many situations that may be thrown your way throughout the process.

Good luck, god bless and all the best in your filmmaking career. Oh, and if you do make it through the ranks and eventually get that

Oscar you've been dreaming of, make sure
you give me a mention (I'm not joking 🙂).

Just remember though, luck will only get you
so far and the film industry is an ever-changing
one - so always have the fluidity and flexibility
to adapt and react to changing audience
requirements if you need to. Remember that
your craft should be ever-developing and ever-
strengthening to make you the best you can
possibly be.

I can't wait to see what you come up with - and
I hope I'll be hearing from you very soon.

References

[1] https://core.ac.uk/download/pdf/46712683.pdf

[2] https://filmmakermagazine.com/49862-independent-filmmaking-passion-or-profession/

[3] https://indiefilmhustle.com/filmmaking-quotes/

[4] http://www.screenwriting.com/wp-content/uploads/how-to-write-a-screenplay-workbook-final.pdf

[5] https://www.aprilyvettethompson.com/uploads/4/1/6/4/41647061/ayt_screenwriting_template_workbook.pdf

[6] http://pages.ucsd.edu/~bgoldfarb/cogn21w10/screenplay-ppnotebook.pdf

[7] http://www.suitedandbooted.org/wp-content/uploads/2014/04/The-3-stages-of-production_-explained.pdf

[8] https://www.cctvcambridge.org/sites/default/files/forms/2preproduction.pdf

[9] https://indiefilmhustle.com/5-stages-indie-film-production/

[10] https://www.oma.on.ca/en/contestpages/resources/free-report-cinematography.pdf

[11] https://www.studiobinder.com/blog/film-lighting-techniques/

[12] http://thecinematheque.ca/education/wp-content/uploads/2012/02/LanguageofFilm07.pdf

[13] http://postproduction.pbworks.com/f/09+Post+Prod+Handbook.pdf

[14] https://www.raindance.org/the-13-steps-of-post-production/

[15] http://thecinematheque.ca/education/wp-content/uploads/2012/02/post-production02.pdf

[16] https://www.bfi.org.uk/sites/bfi.org.uk/files/downloads/uk-film-council-a-filmmakers-guide-to-distribution-and-exhibition-2001.pd